CIRCADIAN

Also by Joanna Klink

THEY ARE SLEEPING

CIRCADIAN

Joanna Klink

PENGUIN POETS

PENGUIN BOOKS
Published by the Penguin Group
Penguin Group (USA) Inc., 375 Hudson Street, New York, New York 10014, U.S.A.
Penguin Group (Canada), 90 Eglinton Avenue East, Suite 700, Toronto, Ontario, Canada M4P 2Y3
(a division of Pearson Penguin Canada Inc.)
Penguin Books Ltd, 80 Strand, London WC2R 0RL, England
Penguin Ireland, 25 St Stephen's Green, Dublin 2, Ireland (a division of Penguin Books Ltd)
Penguin Group (Australia), 250 Camberwell Road, Camberwell, Victoria 3124, Australia
(a division of Pearson Australia Group Pty Ltd)
Penguin Books India Pvt Ltd, 11 Community Centre, Panchsheel Park, New Delhi – 110 017, India
Penguin Group (NZ), 67 Apollo Drive, Rosedale, North Shore 0745, Auckland, New Zealand
(a division of Pearson New Zealand Ltd.)
Penguin Books (South Africa) (Pty) Ltd, 24 Sturdee Avenue, Rosebank, Johannesburg 2196, South Africa

Penguin Books Ltd, Registered Offices:
80 Strand, London WC2R 0RL, England

First published in Penguin Books 2007

1 3 5 7 9 10 8 6 4 2

LIBRARY OF CONGRESS CATALOGING IN PUBLICATION DATA
Klink, Joanna, 1969–
Circadian / Joanna Klink.
p. cm.—(Penguin Poets)
ISBN 978-0-14-303884-9
I. Title.
PS3561.L5C57 2007
811'.6—dc22 2006052761

Printed in the United States of America
Designed by Ginger Legato

Whatever the landscape had of meaning appears to have been
    abandoned,
unless the road is holding it back, in the interior,
where we cannot see

—Elizabeth Bishop, "Cape Breton"

ACKNOWLEDGMENTS

BOSTON REVIEW *Sea by Dusk, Winter Field*

THE CANARY *Sea by Flowers*

CITY ART JOURNAL *Excerpts from a Secret Prophecy, Hourglass*

COLORADO REVIEW *Studies for an Estuary, Draftsmanship, Fisherman, Flicker, Farm Soil, Auroras*

COLUMBIA: A JOURNAL OF LITERATURE & ART *Sea Ice, Beehive, The Eventides*

CROWD *Day Window*

DENVER QUARTERLY *Raven*

FENCE *Prism*

GULF COAST *Mariana Trench*

THE IOWA REVIEW *Whoever like you and all doves (three poems)*

JUBILAT *Sea Levels*

THE KENYON REVIEW *And Having Lost Track, Thoughts on Fog*

THE LAUREL REVIEW *Vireo*

NEW AMERICAN WRITING *Should I call it mechanical, Forgetting the northern sun, And when I asked*

NEW ORLEANS REVIEW *Antelope*

POETRY NORTHWEST *Blue Ice*

PLOUGHSHARES *Apology*

POST ROAD *River in Dusk, Shooting Star*

SMARTISH PACE *Porch in Snow*

SONORA REVIEW *Four Messages*

WILDLIFE *Grassfield*

And Having Lost Track, Porch in Snow, and *Mariana Trench* are reprinted from LEGITIMATE DANGERS: AMERICAN POETS OF THE NEW CENTURY, edited by Cate Marvin and Michael Dumanis (Sarabande Books, 2006).

Apology is reprinted from ISN'T IT ROMANTIC: 100 LOVE POEMS BY YOUNGER AMERICAN POETS, edited by Brett Fletcher Lauer and Aimee Kelley (Verse Press, 2004).

Day Window is reprinted from THE PIP GERTRUDE STEIN AWARDS FOR INNOVATIVE POETRY IN ENGLISH: 2005–2006, edited by Douglas Messerli (Green Integer, 2006).

Excerpts from a Secret Prophecy is reprinted from LONG JOURNEY: CONTEMPORARY NORTHWEST POETS, edited by David Biespiel (Oregon State University Press, 2006).

Porch in Snow, *Antelope*, and *Winter Field* are reprinted from MONTANA WOMEN WRITERS: A GEOGRAPHY OF THE HEART, edited by Caroline Patterson (Farcountry Press, 2006).

Sea by Dusk, *River in Dusk*, *Sea Levels*, and *Shooting Star* are reprinted from THE IOWA ANTHOLOGY OF NEW AMERICAN POETRIES, edited by Reginald Shepherd (University of Iowa Press, 2004).

Grateful acknowledgment to the University of Montana and to the Rona Jaffe Foundation.

Thank you to my family for their immense support.

Thank you Paul Slovak, Allen Grossman, Beth Murray, Kelly Barry, and John D'Agata. Thank you Matt McGowan and Erik Herzog. For help with my eyes, thank you Karin Stallard, Nan Dunne, and Marina Zaleski.

To my students at the University of Montana, my gratitude and amazement.

For Baker and our time together, abiding love.

CONTENTS

CIRCADIAN

for Robert Baker

AURORAS

It began in a foyer of evenings
The evenings left traces of glass in the trees
A book and a footpath we followed
Under throat-pipes of birds

We moved through a room of leaves
Thin streams of silver buried under our eyes
A field of white clover buried under our eyes
Or a river we stopped at to watch
The wind cross it, recross it

Room into room you paused
Where once on a stoop we leaned back
Talking late into daylight
The morning trees shook off twilight
Opening and closing our eyes auroras

Beyond groves and flora we followed a road
Dotted with polished brown bottles,
Scoured furrows, a wood emptied of trees

It was enough to hollow us out
The evenings left grasses half-wild at our feet
Branches with spaces for winds

The earth changes
The way we speak to each other has changed
As for a long while we stood in a hall full of exits
Listening for a landscape beyond us

[handwritten annotation: metonymy for birdsong! metaphor birds throat is a pipe]

DAY WINDOW

Into the kitchen a thread of sun
floats down quiet. A private
sense of absence in my
everyday patterns—breath
pulled into my ribs prying
me apart—and outside
the window coated in soot
from winds that came
all winter, some process has
ceased—although birds
drop and lift off the roof,
aerial sweeps, or just bursts of
feather, wings, claws, and the leap
of heart I would have,
should I be so brightly altered
with the chances of life,
a reparation I feel gathering
in the pitch, scarlet wing, most
unnatural sound held in the dim
threshold of my throat—
or am I less than I was—
and fear I can't distinguish
the thin blue current inside the light
from the slant in my voice
or the early morning fog laid over
the grass from the voice
that underlies everything.

RIVER IN DUSK

What wind there was
What sky there was was not
enough, I could not
hear beyond a cry a signal
beautiful idea to touch
you or wince where
faint against the glass you
sensed my hand—umbra ~~shadow~~
icy with bells—how
in the answer we felt
a sweeping diminishment
of things, fleets
of noise, faraway
wash of sequoias, and separate,
clouded, flat, haunting
river-surfaces torn in cool
air against the late
afternoon
Who told you *time will come*
Who finally seized the wind-rills
dragging aqueous regions inside
And inside the warrant
And inside the indifference through which
you are invited to pass, what
would occur in the half-second of
your leaning to
speak me that music
(Isn't it better to *live*)
You are right here
You are part of my persuasion

APOLOGY

Lately, too much disturbed, you stay trailing in me
and I believe you. How could I not feel
you were misspent, there by books stacked clean on glass,
or outside the snow arriving as I am still arriving.
If the explanations amount to something, I will tell you.
It is enough, you say, that surfaces grow so distant.
Maybe you darken, already too much changed,
maybe in your house you would be content where
no incident emerges, but for smoke or glass or air,
such things held simply to be voiceless.
And if you mean me, I believe you.
Or if you should darken, this inwardness would be misspent,
and flinching I might pause, and add to these meager
incidents the words. Some books
should stay formal on the shelves.
So surely I heard you, in your complication aware,
snow holding where it might weightless rest,
and should you fold into me—trackless, misspent,
too much arranged—I might believe you
but swiftly shut, lines of smoke rising through snow,
here where it seems no good word emerges.
Though it is cold, I am aware such reluctance
could lose these blinking hours to simple safety.
Here is an inwardless purpose.
In these hours when snow shuts, it may be we empty,
amounting to something. How could I not
wait for those few words, which we might enter.

DRAFTSMANSHIP

Draftsmanship, what we once called
desire. A black quality of light within
the clouds, the shadows filtering like wind
around each outline—this poor stack of twigs,

a hanging wire looping toward the earth.
I speak to you because I do not know you,
and having lately made waste of what I care for,
understand certain things will not be possible—

to hold a season back. A sheaf of flowers
extends into space, vinegar and glass,
the sharp beginnings of airflow—and I would not ask
more of you, an immensity in the small print of

spring, skinny branches almost yellow
at the tips, sun thrown white and nacreous over
these front yards—untraceable adjustments—
and I, too, would have done things differently,

would have sensed that certain attentions
are impossible—you love what delivers you
into light, which sometimes means
to be possessed of a sickness so pure

it feels shapeless—this is the hard way,
knowing we will not meet, knowing
that the blankness you are fighting
is not the same as the one I feel in my flesh

every day—spring rips into the gravel,
the tulips, bright murmuring from the valleys,
this house finch perched on a dirty grout patch,
grazing the air with an absence of sound—

some restless search for new patterning—
eggshell the color of feathers, the color of bone—
and this deep soreness in my eyes—take it
back, all the cures of newness, the blindness

in each next uncovering—and you almost
can't make out the rain falling through sunlight,
and you almost miss the faint lace of green
over these young trees, although I have fought

hard to see, have tried to find some way
around this misshapenness at the center,
the world loved and not loved, two fish
glinting dark-gold beneath the blurred river

surface—have I loved it enough—the pipes
noisy with water, needles of gray rain loosed
to the flowerpots, an attic lit with sun and old
dust—loved it enough—although it was

not possible, my last bookcase collapsed,
aspirin and white paper—everything
shaken open, this selfsame grain across
fields still blistered from long winter,

each placard scrawled with black and white gold,
in place of destroying, in place of dead envy—
and everywhere pulling worth back
into itself, like words held up to the clouds,

memorized and half-forgotten, an element
of ether over which our voices move—*with one
written thing goes the world*—the thread of speech
pulled taut then released into a widening

participation of light and air—what I sought,
what you hoped for—although it was not
possible—loved enough, although not
lived or entered, although not understood.

SEA LEVELS

Dividing time equally between earths, there in the coldness
pulling south, flint in the dusk, a few stars.
You are irreducible, there where you stand,
and all the mountains dropping into water.
To what else would you give such care?
Each thing made in the moment we hear.
I understand when the winds rinse ice across the mountains
and the mountains throw out their rock and burden, and the light
and the feel of the light are the beginning of what we know.
How close can you come?
Come into the world again.
Birds are moving through sky, a few
below roof-level, rising where there are breezes.
One night and division sets in, two and we wonder
what pardon, three and you are sleeping poorly.
Simplicity remembering there never was a time.
There never was a time a time before spacious disquiet.
There never was a below-sea-level where the bird
flew warmly in water. There never were stars
shaking on the surface or stars sinking.
The fish dream as the stars fall past them.
The bird seeks a place to land and cannot, in the swell of tides,
in the shallow sandstops, find it. All freedoms
drawing us forth. The flocks of geese
swim in the sand-flecked night, and bring stories of arrival.

GRASSFIELD

At dusk they ease into the fields, having woken from
incomplete dreams, bending their spines to the grasses now

heavy with spring fog. Their arrival is earthless
above the lakes where minnows flex in reedy water

and the soft thin skulls of terns tilt as if in question.
Perhaps you will not recognize them all at such a threshold,

after the winter molt, spread in each direction from an un-
placeable center, their limbs hard-fought against the thawing ground,

gripped like the gravel road by unspecific tremors,
and *hush* and *who* and the black shadow-flickers against

the grasses that extend beyond this everyday hour on earth.
We come to you weak, in need of constant defense,

asking for pardon, salvage, having borne this landscape
too lightly, for some understanding no longer possible,

as when you know you have crossed a boundary and cannot
return. Old world, world into which I was born,

what should I make of the field carrying us both,
the persistent exchange of wood for path over the scrabble-

stalks, the mud and acreage, the pollen drifting in our veins
like the clouds that sift and plunge in the eyes of the animals?

ANTELOPE

In the head of a child, the ice holds.
The snow sifts for hours toward the earthline,

a graylight ground with stars. I would have come
without thought to this place, where the present

extends forever into ice, and the seasons, bright-in-
dark, fall on the crystal threshold, a hard frost

driven deep into the lake stretching over the surface
clouds. Sense, memory, the herd arriving in dusk,

ears pricked, without need or recognition, keeping
their openness alive. What were our hopes

when we first heard that it broke—a sound of dust
in the white expanse, their bodies ghosted

where our minds would have them stall.
And nothing came to interrupt injury,

the fir trees motionless under hours of snow,
a silence clean of every concept. They came

because they believed they would be held,
as in each moment there is no hint of future pain.

First visible animal of the dusk, sleek shape
full of omissions, you are allowed to pass.

All day the snow fell. Around the lake, the air
filled with moths, light as pencil outlines.

AND HAVING LOST TRACK

And having lost track, I walked
toward the open field. Now transparent,
now far, the day-moon burned through the waste
air. I passed a scientist, his hands
holding cinders to the sky.
I passed a pile of corroding metal,
a young girl with a ring of keys.
The sound of a flute came and went.
I passed a garden under snow, a half-open book,
a man unaccustomed to grief.
And thought: what must I do differently.
And could not avoid the scraps of glass,
the fog at my knees. I, like you,
am irreparable. And aware that
when the cold clouds lift, there may be nothing.
And having lost track, I walked by the high
gold grasses, a softness I could not reach to
feel. And came upon a table laid out
with wine and winter shadow. We shall
grow heavy. And felt the signature of light,
of sound and people, laid bare within me.
And I would give it up: this weight,
this concentration. Would gladly
be mistaken, or rebuild by force what
cannot hold. I passed the slow autumn sun
as it moved through the branches,
the terrible spread of deserts, the leap
of a bleeding deer.
To be outside the classifiable world,
and having lost track, and having heard
no message. As when a single existence
vanishes and the flute does not warp,
or sounds like the inside of a shell,

bright
red
~~cool~~ sun

12

and the word for shell means
too many things. As if this were the last
mile, a path fashioned with white roses.
And chose the science of extraction,
the science of snow.
And walked in the dark world,
everywhere shaking with light.
That we only exist. That we do not
have the means. And are free to take place.

PORCH IN SNOW

There you are, snow filling the air,
in the midst of silence. The porch still with ice
and the distances shifting in us,
snow falling in clouds to the streets.
Winter, there is no prayer but this,
to hold fast in the time of few choices.
An animal moves through the backyards, its eyes
precise and lit, the premise of everything I believe,
a whiteness that measures the sadness
of the creature unsure where it will sleep.
And every conviction you held of what it means
gone, the evening long gone. And it may be
a shining in your eyes as other sleepers enter homes.
Restless with ice, an animal crosses the wide field
in you, a darkness that asks
everything for measure, spacious world,
the animal moves against all winter,
a grace of feeling we had not imagined.
This also comes into the winter garden
while a car starts, snowlight falling across the alley
in radiant extension of everything I cannot
see. As if the night were utterly changed,
as if you would turn to enter the rooms again,
lit against cold, and there were no further sorrow
possible for you, in any form.

VIREO

And although I am afraid for the soil and silver hills,
for the root systems and breath systems, for those

who feed under cover of night, there is still a strange
borderless joy in the upper rooms of trees, as vireos

sail between branches, bobbing through the swept
white sky, acquainted with cloud-drift and the evermore

intricate breezework of space. A reverie
of hollow bones and strong taut feathers that whisk and

pivot with our eyes' vitality, they elude each specific death
as hawks move like light through smoke, hanging without sound.

Innocents, the day has brought you everything you need,
and the depths that open up beneath you are of no

concern to you—the phlox growing up the rotting shed,
the slow scuttle of cars, each hometown blinking through

exhaust as the evening broods then descends.
We fail where you most survive, at the brink of air, pushing

hard against the pressures of the given. What do you
have, coming suddenly where all things are?

BLUE ICE

And though we may know nothing of each other,
we have to do with one another, also the dark washing

quiet of certain tides. Along the north-coasts the blue ice
sinks and wavers, and the watermarks rise at all the ports of call

as farther south a skiff moves briskly over waves,
loosening some wintriness beneath the slow bewilderment of

clouds. And the pale blue beryl waters, the emeralds
and other beryls, the natural blue stones below the supple

waterstones, and the evanescence of sea through light
that separates all the colors of daylight from their mineral luster,

the new grasses on the beaches, the plusher greens they portend—
even the gray-and-speckled-greens of human eyes—

my songs, I would find all the names for blue and banish
each etcetera, undertaking to live where the world

richly dissolves in its departures, the estuaries sliding to sea-
floors, the doorways where a hand is quickly clasped,

or the pods ripped from the shaking milkweed stalks,
the plume agates and flower agates and flowers half-sketched

over the blotched and furrowed farmland, and the bones
heirloomed beneath the lilac roots, the gypsum flakes

that flash from this black dirt in whose fire we turn—
and everything we thought we were, wandering

a long time through our lives, might count, might help
guide us—since we have not been spared.

RAVEN

Snow, pure blue, tissue and blood at dusk
moving through the long season of darkness.
The bird a steadiness of cold that arrived months ago

with the killing frost, black wings spectral above
the abandoned buildings, ushering in some code
to be broken or contested. Flies along the boundary

where weather begins, the screen of clouds holding
the pollen of ten thousand species of flowering plants,
incalculable specks of dust forming as they fall

snow crystals, flies, husk of bone and throat,
lure of another life. As if the wind
never blew. As if the woman entering

the factory at five never pulled her coat around herself
and shuddered. Floating six hours through air
yet not dissolved in air, the snow crystal borne

in its slow collapse, nitrate of silver, an ice-print
on the current not once apparent in this night sky:
and the polestar, blurring at intervals into darkness,

and the bare shifting of leaves above which the wolfbird
comes quietly. Comes as the cold air sinks,
as the wine in the wineglass rocks a little,

held to the mouth, comes through snows, along telephone
and tension lines, warehouses and church steeples,
a presence that holds all things in question,

and how far we extend—a bird beyond what can be
touched. The saints at the entryway are worn
and a bit remote. A man waits at the heavy door.

*

And in this way I lifted myself with great effort,
blackened, sent forth in the gray dawn
to simply remain alive, a man who minutes ago

sat on a chaise of bleached print-roses,
a chemist sorting through a heap of clothes.
A birdcall spreads, beads on an abacus—

waxwings bursting from the brush
in the seconds before the coal-light returns.
And the messages go through them, fleet of wings

creating depths and surfaces in air, to what country
do *you* belong, you who have been shipwrecked on earth,
cinched by routine and incapable of eluding injury,

illuminant against the steady gray. The hour
passes. The scavenger flies above what we can bear,
shearing meat from bones, solitary hallucination

between the arctic beats of air, moving scar
over the ravines, the red moon, this bled
wilderness we are turning away from,

the tap of city lights in our chests,
cells dissolving into a fine inner gauze kept hidden,
secure, beyond all violation, having grown silent

in the fleece of night snow, having understood
nothing. The factory fills, empties.
The men play cards far into the night.

*

Raven, most vital, oil on the wings
of difficult flight, as if the north could relax un-
steadily around you. As if some truce were sought

in your endless destination, a child stepping
over the rail-tracks wearing a collar stitched with flowers,
a tightening in the throat of the proprietor—

litter of men and women moving through
the cordage-gloom, rings of weightlessness
forming always at their lips, *raven*, rune

or proof that we are made of temporary boundaries—
each awkward call bearing mercy and news—
and I think I have felt you all along,

wrapped in moving air, looking on the darkness
with uncleared power, each body below in ruin,
the snow cinders brushing the cement,

then gone—ruse that we are, dim contrast
to your negotiations of wind, elegant spine of change
raveling like the voice held open, and the door held open

for the sanctuary to shine upon the one who asks,
in innocence, to see a light beyond the body
where none can be promised, who walks into the street

and feels hungry, having visited the noon-outposts
and the trails, having listened many nights
for the message to come clear, like your dark eyes

creating a sketch of the scarcely human,
a warning where I see your attributes abide in me,
where the world vanish and your black form

behold our species with eyes unopened, that pain
not be substitute for life, that the cycle of days
appear as many choices, or the man

who walks beneath the flashing silt of stars
sense the archway of night rise from the rubble snow
and feel, in blue-black air, himself begin.

SEA BY DUSK

Comes to gather you from clocks and says *be moon,*
be progress. Gathers the bitter fact of chance and says
change in every way. Depending on the harvest,

a heat wave glassed in August, depending on the sea.
Shatters the lullaby, lush and drugged, that would settle
in the downcast reaches. *You who bear a light in you*

bear a compass, unending corrosion, an irreparable
white meadow. Gather what voyage you can,
rhythms emptied in the flutter of Pacific, *without limit,*

a human sound breaking hard against this air,
says *listen become* in the spun fluency of waves.
Sleep, saline, gathers the currents of blue driftwood,

says a hymnal loose with eiderdown and flight—
and comes to prize you in the hour of undertaking,
your new and precise fear. Listen, lean,

that you might feel, in the warm blurring of waves,
the opening and closing of flowers, a circadian call
that pulls each desolation toward clearing,

be ready, be shirred, task of dusk, cadence of star
and constancy, *change,* dropping far in pressured water,
sails of shadow *change in every way.* As in the halls of sky

the swallows gather up whole acres of past error,
vision into vision, printed in the last white sun
spilled out across the tides, your arms, gathered and withstood

in such arcades of stars and sleeping fish, within, without,
pulling near—issued in calligraphies of brine on darkness,
turn, return. We are drifting out of phase, lost, calendar-

sprung, and feel the wings slanting through air
above these fleeting museums of the sea, held
within a single note that moves in pain, pattern,

scarcity and abundance, *abide, turn and return*,
some small far happiness—and the nocturne grows
within each drowsy marine creature, rope, tack,

slowing muscle of the heart, depending on the tides,
depending on the air, a simple mammal stillness
beneath all flights of caution, the net cast far into

space, *who*, clock, stopclock, falling lace, narrow and slow
across the sand-lit skin, in the slipping borders,
your body, *shall be safe*, unscheduled beyond

the sea-torn cemetery, muddy fields, the gardens,
as in a true response to daylight, here, unearthed
in cooling water, moving countries of fish

and floating grass, your hopes, receding
terror, recognize you, it says, *no
loneliness*, no more loneliness

MARIANA TRENCH
35,827 feet

Palpable, principal, unearthly, is alive. Marianas, a stillness gathering

in the unrecognizable deep, cumulative, pressured, like pleasure again and

again ripped from a body. A look you give me, broken understanding,

and you know it will take hours, networks of words to begin again,

kettle and tray, pull of the pupil as it takes in my protests, hopes,

span of shoulders, the gauze of heat and oil on these arms, birds grazing

sheets of surface burning over the trench, as if to trespass for seconds into

the blackness below, an endless inwardness beneath the bright explosions

of their wings, now gliding in some far sense of air, a limit bathed in dusk

leaning beachward, some trust in coast at the end of day when the sweater

pulled over skin still pulses with sun, flowers set in sills to gather light

as a hand passes over the serrated stems, bending and diving

in the summery breeze, sorting through conflict or simply given to motion,

my body shut in your arms, refusing conclusion, feeling the bones spread

beneath skin, an apology forming near the boundary, tense, lost, veins

full of salt-vapor, the story undisclosed, descending in the blue-grays

of your eyes, the slow spread of depth toward some unfelt soundless

sediment, and unraveling toward sea, in need, in everything we can spare.

SHOOTING STAR

Nova, pure periphery, cast into the immobile black, a few blazing

dispatches from abroad, streaks of glass trailing white in the commonplace

hour, autonomous, available in the beds of stars and interrupted councils,

argument of the untended topiary, their animals rising in shapes unintended

to move, though we suffer distinction, and at the hand of the shadow-marvels

the promontories sail, and still mistake the morning's garden-immobility,

birches once fluent with yellow light, that what was sent here is altered,

what was witnessed casual, terraced into the available, shapes of love

or maybe only shapes in the bed, single star streaking in cracked silence

above our argument, casual, intended to move, intended to harbor light,

though we hurt each other, and failing this witness mistake fluency,

some cry obscured in the bed beneath my answer, bearing the old autonomies,

to interrupt our sky's night-flying council which, threaded and glittering,

could make us, in the sudden prescription of that dropping line of

light, still, or simply quiet, and cease in time to be ourselves.

PERIPHERIES

Fisherman

What if, the net drew deep,
all your hours spent in
fractions, the trawler,
beside the wind carrying a thin
snow, holds close to the crude
shores, there were transport,
like other paths painful,
above the gray sea ice
clouded with crystals I felt,
a grim reminder of something
gone wrong, vowels
saltless and scoured, marking
a period of time, a winter,
dragged once against the
beaded sediment, a moment
perceived as purposeless, this
loose bed of perception lifting
through silence the seawater-
fog, the boat, bearing the pressure
of human contact, how
by heat or cold you,
ensured at last, some great
need, having barely opened
your mouth, stood, heart flying

Flicker

Is there no simplicity
in repair, having asked
all the wrong questions,
a flicker in the ever-
greens I say to you in
foreground, thoughts, its
spine settled against brisk
heartbeats, suet and gravel,
a world full of things no longer
nested, something I must
accept, of a piece, beaded
or sensate like words become
much confused, indebted
again to what unexpectedly
leaps out, you are
nobody's star, tiny part of
everything imperceptible
scissors and pins in the
feathered treetops what
will make you safe,
brushing the wood-
pile unseals in the nerve
endings a faint peace

A

maternity
safe

|| also injuries
sitting on scissors &
pins *]*

Sea Ice

There is proof you have
misunderstood, if,
among rough wind-
blinking lights, you refuse
change, steam pulling off
the ice, the marina under
starwash, you said,
you must be willing to
return to sorrow, in
the act of love silent,
long bones, bits of gold and
ligament, and find only
yourself again. Wishbone of
perceptible existence I am
lost to you through desire
of the unspecific, what
persists in the gray ice
floes, or, where you arc
into me, patches of heat,
the sea the earth the ice,
my love of snowdusk moving
in flickers through your
arms, fluid crystal,
you hold in me things
that are not here

Prism

When held against glass,
on the edge of outline,
you would bring me, lilac
flowers, glazed, papery
shapes unhooked from
warm blue I am lost
again, subtracted
from the radiant, as if,
in the middle of a
feeling, something watery,
humid, and gray took
hold, you are, in these unstable
scales of terror, the only
ending I intuit, red
scarf on the street, sparse,
bright rain that falls around
your resting heartbeat,
for no one loves this
world who cannot be
damaged, hard carmine and
quartz, all the injury in
color, you stack, mint,
needle, thermos and
tin, as if, in being
near to them, I might
come to glow

Farm Soil

And in the smallest
kingdoms you find, air
tender against the walled
lungs, calf and foot, what
was done poorly has been left
alone, over the farms,
the bones packed with
flowers, a mercy so easily
damaged I have no notion,
how it was ever
otherwise, you told me,
before you fell asleep, pull
back, each day more
diminished, there is still,
hours later as I leaned
over to feel between your
heartbeats the noonday
bluffs, in the snowbanks
wind that smells of earth, love
even here strains against un-
endurable disappointment

Beehive

Yet could I assure you,
within such broken
systems, bees in the granary
sweet and damp, your eyes
fogging too, I am,
in the inner rooms of
words, ice-colored and
crooked, a little free,
l'abeille, as if in the summer
blush there were meanings
constantly misapprehended,
each time stunning us a-
new, so that what stands
between my self and
the world is mostly you,
compelling in me, despite
the coal-smoke less than
an hour away, some rich
insect happiness against
a life come to nothing,
the petty senseless aims
you say, in such heat the mist
shining if the route were
wrong, still something has been
passed through

WINTER FIELD

What better witness than this evening snow,
its steady blind quiet, its eventual
completeness, a talc smoothing every surface

through the lumen tricks of ice.
No one who comes here hastens to leave,
though the mineral winter makes a dull

math of cold inside the bones, a numbness
thinning into each fingertip and eye.
Faint injury traveling toward earth

in shifting silence, a softness in the weather
passing through us, dark moods of snows—
a sense of peace so deep we extend out

into the blackness of our lives, dread and failure,
and feel no hint of terror, only the premonition
of drift-design, the stars behind the snow

burning in ancient immanence over the field.
What lights a world gone blank with despair?
You were here once; you will be here again.

THOUGHTS ON FOG
for the realist

Fog-locked for three weeks we breathed the haze that hung on trees and
        hooped the mountain-town, a valley pooled with the stuff of

nothing. A hand could slide through a heap of sidewalk-fog and—
        briefly—retrieve itself. Fog in the mouth, across the tongue,

fog in the bronchi, owl-gray abrasions, an air so cinderthick no
        deepening was possible—no place to leave to.

Where will you go?

————————————

       When the cold fell a fog-frost beaded the weed-
stems and faintly feathered the tree-tips. Imperceptibly a pattern

began to make itself felt—the gravel, the fat brown sparrows that never
        returned to our feeder—everything wants to be scarved in ice,

everything wants to be hallowed.

————————————

       This was *never true*. The seconds that pass
pass at your expense, and vaguely one day you find yourself

hardened and the stiff films of tree-lace gone. Where did you go?
       While you were away

————————————

the early dark-of-early winter entered
each thing and burrowed in. A tinge of ink in the red pickup

with its obscene tires, a blackening tint to the air that spooks the empty
houses then spreads its soot-silt across lowering clouds,

the bright-white sky-streaks above those walking home pushed
back by the aerial night. These

are no imagined sorrows. You are the light of the world with me
who have also felt a heaviness gather in the present hour

and against all confusion stepped

———————————

onto a backroad daily exposed to the sun's
fierce and incremental shuffle, where strange balls of fleece

(sheep) stare and dry clouds pass shadow-ponds over dead grass.
Here is space also to grow attached to surfaces, the way seaweeds

hold to those bathed by water (the undersides of boats, ropes, piers),
to feel (at the same time!) sixteen waxwings in the juniper

and the moon glint across the mountain's mica veins.
Here is the real world

———————————

given in exchange for that illusion of weather you call *life*
or *the way things are* and should you find it can't sustain you

(or you miss the wry urban chatter or the concrete plums in the fridge)
      you can leave whenever you like—I'll stay with the mutable fish,

—————————————

the parking lot that was ten thousand years ago a sea,
      the seaweeds (which bloom here and have roots) and yard-weeds

and two women laughing, clutching wet paper bags as their eyes
      leap with cold, each heart beating against the heart-of-

fog or ice or smoke-still
      night. Snow-bits make fine nets in their hair.

THE EVENTIDES

You find yourself in complaint in a field of

lodestone   This is the human way

Shut of day and its soft-colored float glass

you too are shutting   a slow river of stones

underfoot in the grass   The green way the gray way

vesper as the eyelids snow over in dusk

And the field in which you stand   a plinth

to the wavering night   unwitnessed   fathomless

full blind then full dark   Are you never

enough as you are   knowing the night drops and coils

where you speak should you say anything

Your complaint that you were there at all

Anything is less than this   where eventide

and its vacant grasses make a lustrous vacancy

in you   make you remember you were *there*

Remember that you lived   were helped and loved

Who knows what you are   Headlands islands

needles stacked in star-shapes guided by the gem's

crystal structure   Dark-in-rain   a water

unlike any other water   you walk across lands

spread with bones and dust because of you

Because of you the world is warmer   the lake-winds warmer

drafts of dry air that wind over corundum

Because this is all you are offered and it dries out

withdraws   In inches and degrees

you draw into your ownmost ghostliness

shaped into rain and rain-quiet and the quiet

of each seed in each seedpod   Feldspar

morganite   your islands stars in the soil of what was

possible   This then was a shape   a life

a moment given to the world during the world's

brief passing   You are all that you are

You are dayborn   abalone   open to the stars

You find silence in you   Within you

the stars are strange   blurs of shell skeined

with the sliding tides   A horizon always in your eyes

dayborn   born of quiet into quiet   a boat to bear you

piecemeal over unclear water   An immense

emptiness dropped   a sack of dust in dust-gold

cast and scattered   asterial   a salt born in all quiet

through waves of quiet drawn to shore

Nightborn   you are part of everything

you want no part of   Solar   aster   swimmer

you find piecemeal the world within you

and move   shoredrawn daydrawn

as if nothing were asked of you

To approach this shore is to know you are borne

you are asked   the earth waits for you

SEA BY FLOWERS

And what can you tell me of the foothills
spread with dusk, inchoate premonitions of stars
burning low upon this path sloping to the Adriatic.

Out of an earth that cools to scavengers you are made
remote again. Warm smoke from homes a presage
of what we have begun: the shallow seawaves drawn back

so that, on the darker inward water, an ancient calenture
might center itself. And we wish to pass close,
as when a reefless wind rises up from that water,

dispatched as the dusk is briefly dispatched.
Traveler, show me some place where I matter least,
a shoreline as it arches toward horizon close as

attention, always turned to you, sweet in your soundproof
movement, gold-cordovan glow. Surrounding these small houses
built by water, half-heard beneath the corrugated roofs,

a choir of prisms and reeds that seem to extend
from the softening soil in looms of flowers,
each hope distilled in the landscape that is offered.

In the distance someone crosses these bluffs that lift
like dark cathedrals, clearing the astral corridor as it rushes forth,
and in the pipes in the seaside town the water stills,

and at the windows the men, it may be, hesitate.
Little sounds are soundless now. Come down
into the waves in their perpetual shifting inlay,

foaming indigo with night, prospects of wings and snow
uninterrupted around your ankles. Here is the cello ocean,
estranged from the disaster you felt deeply

upon waking, clouding and vitreous, a black moving glass
that holds light, disperses light, poor parable of alabaster
and milky fish, an unmoored country by which we are sustained,

emptied, made rib and filament within a living surfeit of
desire. Would I not have walked these roads
to hold you? Open to me

your arms. The waves slip back in their fluttering silver fringe.
We have slipped into a demand made beautiful,
voiceless, shaking like candlelight against our skin,

oh my beloved. This floating firmament, the wooden boats
returning to their homes, the holding in
of all these breaking things.

FOUR MESSAGES

Reclining with twine
in the scattered shade.
The field mice made notches

    in the bark above the whorled
    mosses—someone is

looking for you.
Aviate-names, tokens,
signs filled the old maple's summer-
chambers. My eyes
lifted too.

    There is not yet
    anything you believe in, dis-
    criminate one, leaping
    from knot to knot
    with your bony hands.

*

A trace of wind in the morning snow.
The quartz forest. Tree-alphabet-tine.
Who-knows-what

    called faintly out to me and
    with my hands I called back.
    No one else was on the path

but the snow-gulches
on either side gathered in a
strong indifferent persistent
order. Yet would not cease to love.

*

It was neither winter nor spring.
Mud fluted the field where we walked

    in no discernible direction.
    You parsed the streams:
    temporary. Outgrown.
    Bliss, loss—you closed

each coverlid. Can this be
the meaning of all the years
of my life? There is

    another world—I can
    think in it. Casting design
    in the marl-sludge-underfoot.
    Every footprint-to-be blazing
    in unscathed outcomes.

Beads of snow-water
slid down the reeds. Each
surface grew looser and
meant more things.

*

Should I listen to you? Bitter mouth
of pronouncements—not a hope,
not a poem.

      I shook the tree and out fell
      a caucus of flowers, twig-dust,
      curtains of aurora.

After a few minutes, a bunting.

      The ground below turned
      to earth and the earth to waves
      and the waves into scarp-
      stones from which a wild air blew
      into both our eyes—stunned us.

And who would we tell.
And for what.

EXCERPTS FROM A SECRET PROPHECY

You who never turned from me,
who were near from the start.
And when I found no prospect of change,
you pulled the coat around me and said nothing.
And the river moved, a slow crush of ice
through the dark dawn. And it wasn't confusion,
and it wasn't grief in the wind, but something
disordered, an isolation over many seasons,
the presence and withdrawal of light on the sealine,
incongruencies of shells. And everywhere
arising and perishing, the tidal life driven by pattern,
division, imbricate distances of dusk across the lawn,
deep summer, a weight in the air
loaded against our eyes—this world, these backyards—
the sky loose with birds.

Aubade of the northern country where every ocean
is imagined, aubade of sun falling across
the vast migrations, a hint of extinction in each wing,
aubade of the old fairgrounds, the vacant orchards
shifting soundlessly in snow—an inwardness
that belongs to the stars and tides, flickering in circuit
between your breath and the clouds, aubade of clouds,
of reperception and sorrow, dark eyes, inconstancy,
everything I have tried to explain, sparse aubade
of the weekend minutes, wild mint, evenings
when we hear the scrape of moths at screen doors,
and always barn swallows banking in the jewel periphery,
always our skin gathering age, in time to be emptied,
in time scarcely recognized—

Why did we live?
                              Apparitions beneath
the slow turning of stars, distilled in bodies
that bruise even when walking softly, unsafe,
unanswered within a world that does not close
but opens, constantly opens, rain and snow on the river,
these reeds breaking through sheets of ice toward sun—
and the language you choose, and what you have chosen
to say to me each day, your voice returning me
to shadow, snowdrift, the constant messages of air,
sweeping pattern within each breath-note—
wren, bed, person, circumstance—
yours and mine, yours, you
who are so at home in words,
who were lost from the start.

TERRARIUM

Should I call it mechanical
timepiece persisting in the absence of
day a repetition of stars
in the terrarium fluorescent
light I have watched for hours despite
such alertness this tremor
in the plant an apprehension
of suffering what can my hands
do darkness soil or breath I would
trade my hopes to hold
the living thing (we
who complete the world
bear slowly each failure)

Forgetting the northern sun
melting the snowpack I kept
myself within or when I walked
walked quickly there is a bright
machinery in the middle of
day sometimes unalone
on the bridge I have felt
traffic noise tear open
a flower all honor in the gray
scales of fish the invisible
river beneath me arrangements
of ice and moving glass released
from a thrush a single
chord given shape bearing skeletal
joy I could sense the hinge the field
spacious nowhere torn by violets

And when I asked for the sorrow
to stop there was
no answer a sound began
to turn in the air subdued
train on the edge of
town a fume
in my lungs held tight to
my body brushing against
a bit of fur in the vicinity
of ground how many
hours have you stood
here like this having fallen
silent dusk dropping haze-
blue shades to the grass
to be held by something
vast borders stitched
to the disappearing trees
a place I loved so much
blurred animal at the edge
of the field I have waited
uninjured as the others
were injured do you not
answer me I answer you

NORTHERN

With the onset of darkness it calls. The clipped
shapes of the note flair out, somewhere at the woods'

sharp edge, into senselessness. A fine rain
suspended in the air unrelieved. Night-winged,

with large forward-facing eyes and in truth I have
never heard it—though it calls. Though I could

scarcely make it out from the narrow bed,
though a brief rain fell inside the room

and the brushwood miles away made a leaping weir
in the stream and the shape of a swallow dove

over reeds of wheat that swayed, though there was
no wind, somewhere behind its eyes

or brushed the discs of feather on its face
and I could not understand what I had lost,

having not heard it or cared, having moved
through the rooms of this house for several hours,

months, turning off hall-lights or the stove or turning
over in my head what I no longer believed,

unwell but for the whites of my eyes where once
the sun could be seen rising in winter as now it

calls and the call breaks easily in all directions
and slips beneath the hovering maple trees

and I think it must pass over beetles, minerals,
wildflowers and thin bones, over pale-and-dark

needles of pines, highway bridges, boatlights
on muddy rivers and the untallied golds of farm-

fields where seeds float, low piano notes
over lakes of air into which rooted things

rise, and yield, like the arable blues and blacks of
foredawn and the blue tint of the cloth awning

over the man's face turned down to the street in grief,
and had I known I would be so long here

I would have seen that certain rains never
do sink fully into the ground, felt the shape-shifting

speech of leaves was part of who I was and
wondered a little longer about the source

of the rainbed and the two irises suspended in
each of our eyes' black liquid and the flowers

in lake ice in a northern wilderness where an owl,
unable to adjust, unable to open its throat, sings,

regardless of what I thought or had sensed, through such
merciless blankness, ceased to sound long ago.

blankness — no expression or sound

WHOEVER LIKE YOU AND ALL DOVES

drains day from darkness loves

darkness and what grows there.
Only now and then

there appears an opalescence
in the sunken night, the back

of a thieving animal or a man
come to stand in a doorway,

as if a candle held up to
a river might create a quiet

so constant there would be
no need for touch. A man

comes to lean on a door-frame
so late at night that his scarab form

absorbs the windless patter of
trees and leaves a splash of black

where his hand, resting against
the wooden frame, just was.

WHOEVER LIKE YOU AND ALL DOVES
drains evening from

darkness are my sole accompaniment
in early maps of dusk across

the scrubbed slight-rising field.
What simple use my feet are

put to, dissolving for an hour
along the bleached grasses

whose feathered stems begin
to burn in weird yellow-greens

and reds that obscure whole
bolts of low pocked stone.

Nothing I have seen on earth
is so lost as this expanse made

precise in the receding light,
a thousand thousand brittle

stems brushed in audible
reverence to air in whose

surround I am imprinted,
wandering blank spot with limbs

scarring into limestone beds
below thresholds of sense

or clear estrangement, as when,
in the next day's ravaged noon,

sunlight sweeps the prairie
never touching the ground.

WHOEVER LIKE YOU BLUES
weeds at the edge of

this forked street and leaves
skirts of birds in the skeletal

trees, a season's salinity.
Hour within autumn hour-in-

vanishing, the yellow leaves
draw, through dry quiet,

close to the ground.
Below the cool spindrift beds

of seeds lies a subterranean
braille of what will perish

and what grow, an unlivable
meaning beyond measures

of meanings filling with dark
nutrient and root wherein glint

the pressures of everydayness
and harrowed calendar matter,

into whose reaches even
the moon and its opal material

cannot burrow, whose where-
abouts are manifest in the depths

of faces of strangers when they
seem to see through you.

WHOEVER LIKE YOU AND ALL DOVES
sees the baby boy drop stones

in the metal flowerpot and how
quickly they sink through

the water in his eyes or rest
on the rain as do blossoms

he's scraped the dirt to clutch.
What floats in red bits on

the surface stays crushed or
lifts with the pull of another

stone's blurring to the bottom.
Who in such a spell would tell him

no or make in the sand a depthless
map of where he will live

and his sisters with him,
as if the nearby sea were free

of all oblivions I have felt
enter my skull in the afternoons

sunk by steady spring-gray rains.
When the rains come at night

they trample the grass and
the birds we feel in the nearby

olive trees stay silent. Throw it
away or keep it close—the stone still falls

and the clouds just beyond us
drive through the ether he breathes

when he imagines clouds having
not yet learned the word.

Pebbles, years, weathers,
hesitation. The iris stalks taper

later in the day and the dove-
colored walls whiten in cerements

that gather all nearby bodies
into throes of burnished stone.

If there is rain there are marshes.
If there are seas there are bays

and if you say *long-glowing*
you have not said too much—

insuperable futures arriving
in wind-long waves from

the sea—or *steadfast* or
shallow leave him unscathed

where the cities spill brown smoke
and smooth in lavish cements

each path to poverty and rage
as a quorum forms in the dust-

colored streets of winds
that loop over wastes through

tenements and towns carrying
insects and thin plastic cups,

the umber of ancient greening
hills, pigeons, puddles, paper-

litters and wisps of duff
or air from the nearby woods

and the gray animals there,
the words *hardly* and *who*

and the sounds that mean *knell*
and *drill* and the surface tinctures

of arms and unseen disease,
scattershot like the blouse-white

winter curtains of a house
long since abandoned, without ardor

or dismay, and arrives one day
at an arid place where no life

should be, and to no one says
no, says *please*, or *enough*.

STUDIES FOR AN ESTUARY

The study is always lost to deeper ocean.
From a distance the local watermen see approaching winds
as they move across the water, a long abandonment
into current. The winds pull the surface into
arcs and bands, where below it suddenly drops,
a sea-height winding downward, dark with silk.
These are boundaries they do not understand,
why depth is evident only in wind, why the insistence of air
should sweep aside the water in shallow bays and yield nothing.
Where the river enters the larger body
early winter winds break against the sandbars
and pleasure makes it fluent, as far out the seaspray
        passes into light. The bodies of the men
a great space on which an ocean is growing—
a few seabirds swing through air then drop to the surface.
Like the winds, they float on currents and will wait
for warm water to slide beneath them, films of salt
and coralline dust, until they are mostly held, and calmed—

I see always the song-passage as it moves away from me,
        place of sunblue quiet.
I see everywhere the frequent change and the sorry answers.
And still, what promise is this, what poise,
what poise of what worlds.

Perhaps there are two seas,
one below the surface and one above,
and the shapes moving within the water
we recognize only by their darkness.
Bright water streams close around them.
If there is plant life, it moves against this massive current
        into coastal estuary, where it can grow.
The fish are swept seaward, out toward some drifting center
while the men wait, and stare, so among themselves in this cold music
(wind acting on water, water dragging the cloud-patterns out)
and I feel I cannot hold within my body
or abide within a body.
Estuary, entry, light guiding the wave, green-deepening shadow.
And there is always something further than you, liquid,
unlived, and the ocean is widespread, driving away from shore.
And we are always *coast*, are always where we stand,
and the men say *Quiet widen the shoreline breakers*
and the men are subdued by blacker weather washing inward,
sculpting, dissolving the waves, to hold up some
brief sweet concert (bouvardia, breeze, a room letting in clouds)
until I am required to be someone else, and the water follows
        some course perfectly
uninvolved with me.

Why are things as they are, and not some other way?
The stones open.
The gulls stand in their sleep.
The men watch for weather in the passage
beyond the feathered waves in seablue shadow,
beyond the arrangement of this distance, where we fall
        into singleness and fight to understand—
I watch for the song that promises change
and in change the evanescent music
where dusk has gradually appeared, a piece of time,
to lay its spun storm over the water
and the passage hushed now that the rain
has opened over ocean, and though sometimes there is rage,
though sometimes we are involved in things without great care,
the rain still falls and turns glass strands to air,
loosening cords in shapes of wings or islands,
and the men understand, in their preponderance, some history
that abides in water-forms, that reaches deep into our inattention,
and we are constantly given indications, and we are always
        unprepared—a sound,
inconsequential, it may seem, or inhuman,
but imprinted in the voice of precedent, half orchard half waste,
lexicon opening without entry, until the river unwinds
in sail and smoke-gray sky and is made visible:
and the angle at which it is swept back,
and the moving arms of the men, covered in rain,
and the shadows of fish that spread through darker waters.

HOURGLASS

And you stay through the hard hours
when, late in the day, the snow falls,
a single dreamless motion of white sands
hanging toward the blighted shore.
       You who, gathered in such quiet,
understand only some vague prayer for elevation,
here where so many things end—
astral trails of snow, three notes from a song,
the dusk-gray radiance of the breaking surf.
Transitoriness, swift passage of my body's life,
and within this lampblack blindness
the weight of our separate existences,
yours next to mine in murmured unseen waves,
the fire inside the mussel shell that disappears
       when it is opened—whole histories of feeling falling
in luminous virga across estuaries and white earth,
a dust we take into our lungs and exhale,
as in summer the willow releases its drowsy
shapelessness to grass.

Do you shine in the dark.
       Or lean toward the feint of this unbearable sky,
its waves of ice and whitened silt cast over
the great needs of peoples so that there is
no place where completion might just linger,
no pattern so flawless it cannot be laid down,
as tidal salts are dragged by winds
then dropped against black shoals,
that same dense gravity we feel in profound sleep,
the heaviness of hunger over a sea
       white with inner lights—
and what you cannot say, what I cannot think—

that nothing we do or hope or make
holds fast against such un-
relenting steadiness.

If we would stay here, let it be a felt place.
Designed for something more than keepsake.
Gentle, edgeless, with unexpected curves of
clear ascent, as a hand might rise to skim
then touch the dirty window glass, or a shorebird
      lift from thin beach reeds and find its wings
in relation to its body unexpectedly light,
free of complex greed and called beyond
the constant dread of storms, a vein-pulse
passing through icy strands of rain as if through solid matter,
one long dazzling exposure to cloud-and-water-shadow,
      a current gathering and lengthening
in a field of raw blue depths into which,
distinct and flashing,
its small body sinks, or briefly dives.

NOTES

DAY WINDOW
". . . let the bones lie here with their message, for those who might decipher it, if they come down late among us from the stars . . . Perhaps there is no meaning in it at all, the thought went on inside me, save that of journey itself . . . It has altered with the chances of life, and the chances brought us here." —Loren Eiseley, "The Slit," *The Immense Journey*

SEA LEVELS
"I want, as Charles Olson says, to come into the world." —Robert Creeley, "A Sense of Measure," *Was That a Real Poem & Other Essays*

GRASSFIELD
"It is a ridiculous demand which England and America make, that you shall speak so that they can understand you. Neither men nor women nor toadstools grow so. As if that were important, and there were not enough to understand you without them. As if nature could support but one order of understandings, could not sustain birds as well as quadrupeds, flying as well as creeping things, and *hush* and *who*, which Bright can understand, were the best English . . ." —Henry David Thoreau, *Walden*

ANTELOPE
Eighty-five antelope fell through thin ice and drowned on January 9, 2004, while moving south across Fort Peck Lake in Valley County, Montana. Antelope have been making the crossing for hundreds of years.

BLUE ICE
"Those who stand on the crossfront, those who know nothing of one another, have to do with one another." —Martin Buber, "The Validity and Limitation of the Political Principle," *Pointing the Way*

RAVEN
"Living in these ephemeral cloud lands are thousands of species of bacteria, fungi, and protozoa; the pollen of more than ten thousand species of flowering plants; and an incalculable number of specks of dust. Some of these particles will form the nuclei of snow crystals." —Bernard Mergen, *Snow in America*

". . . ravens nest on and even in abandoned buildings, on telegraph and high-tension lines, and on church steeples . . ." —Bernd Heinrich, *Ravens in Winter*

". . . the messages go through them . . ." —Loren Eiseley, "The Bird and the Machine," *The Immense Journey*

". . . the small tap of stars / opening in my body . . ." —Natalie Peeterse, "Madrugada (5)," unpublished poem

SEA BY DUSK
". . . depending on the sea." —Mark Levine, "Island Life," *Enola Gay*

"alone no loneliness in the dream in the quiet / in the sunrise in the sunset Louise." —Linda Gregg, "Alma to her Sister," *Too Bright to See*

"'Patterns / are temporary boundaries,' the moving countries / where nothing / is seen in isolation." —Ronald Johnson, "Four Orphic Poems," *Selected Poems*

MARIANA TRENCH

The Mariana Trench is the deepest spot on earth. "Of all the worlds the abyss alone remains unaltered. It is the one place on the planet where conditions remain as they have been since the beginning, where the five-mile pressures have not altered, where no suns have ever shone, where the cold is the same at the poles as at the equator, where the seasons are unchanging, where there is no wind and no wave . . . This is the sole world on the planet that we can enter only by a great act of the imagination." —Loren Eiseley, "The Great Deeps," *The Immense Journey*

SHOOTING STAR

"Dawn under day, or dawning, lake, late edge, / Assumptive pure periphery where one thrust prominence / Now gives me back my eyes . . ." —Alvin Feinman, "Circumferences," *Preambles and Other Poems*

WINTER FIELD

This poem is for Cameron Paterson.

EXCERPTS FROM A SECRET PROPHECY

"You who never arrived / in my arms, Beloved, who were lost / from the start . . . Who knows? perhaps the same / bird echoed through both of us / yesterday, separate, in the evening . . ." —Rainer Maria Rilke, "[You who never arrived]," *Ahead of All Parting: The Selected Poetry and Prose of Rainer Maria Rilke*, translated by Stephen Mitchell

"And again one asked, not of the past this time, but of the future, there where the winds howled through open space and the last lichens clung to the rock, 'Why did we live?' There was no answer I could hear." —Loren Eiseley, "How Natural is 'Natural'?" *The Firmament of Time*

WHOEVER LIKE YOU AND ALL DOVES

"Whoever like you and all doves drains day and evening from darkness" —Paul Celan, untitled poem, *Speech-Grille and Selected Poems*, translated by Joachim Neugroschel

". . . deer along the dark underside of a hill / a thousand / thousand." —Elisabeth Whitehead, "dialogue," unpublished poem

"Miranda: 'And mine, with my heart in't; and now farewell / Till half an hour hence.' Ferdinand: 'A thousand, thousand!'" —Shakespeare, *The Tempest*

STUDIES FOR AN ESTUARY

"Wind-driven currents sweep larval organisms away from deep ocean waters filled with predators and into coastal estuaries, where they can grow." —Jan DeBlieu, *Wind*

"Each wing-bone and feather has a suite of muscles that can slightly shift its orientation and, in unison, adjust the wing's total geometry—the angle at which it is swept back . . ." —David Campbell, cited in *Wind*

"Time distributes itself, flows away, but to our gain, half orchard, half waste." —René Char, "Arthur Rimbaud," *Recherche de la base et du sommet*

HOURGLASS

". . . the pattern of that wake pulsing between them, those measured unseen waves . . ." —Marianne Wiggins, *Evidence of Things Unseen*

"Because the world is not designed for keepsake." —Marianne Wiggins, *Evidence of Things Unseen*

JOANNA KLINK teaches poetry at the University of Montana. She is the author of one previous book, *They Are Sleeping*, and her work has appeared in *The Kenyon Review*, *Denver Quarterly*, *Boston Review*, and other journals. A recipient of a Rona Jaffe Foundation Writers' Award in 2003, she lives in Missoula.